Erica Jolly

I was born, in Adelaide, the year the Reichstag was burnt down. My first love was history but I turned to literature in the 1970s. Whitlam made it possible for me and people like me to attend university. Money did not come first. I was not burdened with debt for daring to want to learn. My interest in poetry began when I taught in Biggleswade, Bedfordshire. That interest grew with my discovery of the work of Judith Wright. While teaching, I wrote little. When I left the Education Department Elizabeth Mansutti took me to Friendly Street. In the last twelve years my poems, provoked too often by the horrors of a society in which a politician can say sleep deprivation is not a form of torture—sorry 'coercion'—have been published in a number of journals, poetry collections and read on 5UV, now Radio Adelaide. My collection *Pomegranates* (Lythrum Press 2004) has received appreciative reviews, most particularly in the Online Review of Australian Studies, Menzies Centre, London.

Ivan Rehorek

I was born in the middle of the last century in the middle of an island in the middle of a river in the middle of Europe.

So much for symbolism.

I worked in children's theatre for many years (Paperbag Theatre) and now work at Tauondi Aboriginal College as an Art lecturer.

So much for theatre.

My star sign would probably be a Mitsubishi with Radiator ascendant . . . what do you mean it doesn't exist?!

I am Avalanche because I am white and cover plenty of ground and tend to knock things flying and go WHOOOOSH a lot.

My family consists of artists, playwrights, performers, musicians, teachers, herpetologists and veterinaries.

All of the above is perfectly true.

Unruly Sun

Friendly Street Poets 31

edited by
Erica Jolly
and
Ivan G Rehorek (aka Avalanche)

Friendly Street Poets in association with Wakefield Press

Friendly Street Poets Incorporated
in association with
Wakefield Press
1 The Parade West
Kent Town
South Australia 5067

www.friendlystreetpoets.org.au
www.wakefieldpress.com.au

First published 2007

Cover image: Mosaic of the sun by Daisybell Virgin, Tauondi,
photographed by Greg Grace
Designed and typeset in 9/11.5 pt Palatino by Clinton Ellicott,
Wakefield Press
Printed and bound by Hyde Park Press

ISBN 978 1 86254 742 1

Government
of South Australia

Arts SA

Friendly Street Poets Inc. is supported
by the South Australian Government
through Arts SA.

fox creek

Contents

Friendly Street 31
is dedicated to
Rae Sexton
Ray Stuart
and
Maureen Vale

Preface

As the editors of *Unruly Sun*, Ivan and I wish to acknowledge the Kaurna people, the traditional owners and custodians of the Adelaide plains. Fittingly the solar-powered cover of *Unruly Sun* is the work of Daisybell Virgin, an art student at Tauondi, the Aboriginal College. ('Tauondi' means 'to break through'.) We look forward to the time Aboriginal poets feel welcome and accept Friendly Street's invitation to add their voices to our monthly meetings.

* * *

Previous prefaces of *Friendly Street Readers* have provided the historical development of Friendly Street, the longest running poetry-reading centre across Australia. The history of Friendly Street, *Best of Friends*, to be launched in 2007, will deepen everyone's understanding of our growth. We thank the Director and staff of the South Australian Writers' Centre for their support. In *Southern Write* we share our successes with others, find challenges through competitions, express our views of the South Australian writing scene. In the Atrium a significant number of launches have taken place of the work of poets for whom Friendly Street has been an important stepping stone.

Prizes have been offered this year for the best mystical and the best political poem. Peter Eason and Graham Rowlands have been the respective judges. Winning poems have been included in the collection.

What matters most to me is the voice of the poet wherein lies the freedom of the human spirit, too often confined in the 'mainstream'. Think only of the misery of the Murray to know what that means. Therefore, I'm glad I have had the opportunity to work with Ivan—some of Friendly Street saw us as an odd couple—and have shared the infectious enthusiasm evident in his contribution to this preface.

* * *

One of my most beloved lines in poetry goes like this: 'I looked up and saw myself watching me . . .' It has that simple elegance that so moves us, touches the heart and spins our senses. Kind of like the first time you fall in love, I might add.

Here is a selection, then, of such wonderful lines—here you will find lines that sing, lines that howl, lines that dance and lines that slither, lines that tumble with eloquence and lines that go beyond language . . . and all these remind us that Poetry was once called . . . Magic.

Why Unruly Sun?

Well, it reminded us both of several things, among them Yeats' 'dishevelled wandering star . . .' and a much loved poetry textbook, called the *Runaway Sun*, produced right here in Adelaide.

And then, of course, when all's said and Donne (pun intended) there's more said than done.

The editing process was quite wonderful—we both took turns in selecting pieces for each other's delectation, just like at a Chinese banquet.

('Here, Erica, try this, it's a beaut.' 'Ooh, yes it is, isn't it? What do you think of this one?')

* * *

We thank everyone who contributed by reading at Friendly Street, *ArtState* for continuing to publish the poems we chose, Graham Catt for putting the poems on the Friendly Street website, Wakefield Press for its support for the publication and, most particularly, the Friendly Street committee for giving us the opportunity to find our place under our very own Unruly Sun.

Avalanche and Erica

Paper

As delicate
and lovely
as origami

As binding
and precious
as a Ketubah

As bright
and colourful
as confetti

As airy
and dancing
as a lantern

As deep
and uncharted
as a library

As ecstatic
and tender
as a book of love poems:

the blank pages
we have written upon
this first year

David Adès

Passaporto per L'Estero*

In a pocket of cloth
fingers and thumb
read cursive
as if it was Braille:
written in the past;
read in hindsight;
lost to the future

In a pocket of cloth
measurements stand:
sign posts between
truths and half truths.
Scribed in black ink
the thirty year old
casalinga,**
with brown eyes
and short black hair
boards a ship
at Messina
and docks at Fremantle

In a pocket of green,
gold embossed cloth
numbered 5735617P,
the width of a palm;
length of a forefinger,
a woman noted
as holding no other
distinguishing features
bears four children
buries a husband
and now waits
for nightfall

Gaetano Aiello

*foreign passport
**housewife

Quitting

Scratching at my nicotine patch
like an addict without a fix,
I chat and smile with robotic neatness,
envisioning that last time of matches striking.
I twitch and tic and sigh,
outraged by my own undoing,
and longing for the heady sink
the slow burning sickness
the weary bliss,
of that last cigarette.
Huddled on a street-corner shamefully
I blow smoke in the direction of a small child
and I'm embarrassed by my weak willed nonsense.
I long for the days of smoke filled theatres
and unlimited sunbaking
and marijuana for medicinal purposes.
I crave a cigarette packet with a picture of a flower on it.
I long for a world of gluttony without consequence.

Liz Allan

Four Loaves from the Heart's Oven

for sister Eva Sallis

1

Lady of ladies in the cities of distrust
Lady of ladies
Between the shores of earth and sky
There is a bridge of certainty

2

When the glass is empty
The orchard emptied of its shadows
And the waterwheel is empty
And when the garden of words and letters has lost
The lilies of meaning
Then I will fill them with an abundance of desires
And with the prayers that flood
From my heart to my tongue

3

I built in my imagination
A minaret
And a playground with swings
And I embroidered the deserts
With fountains that played in orange groves
And when I fell asleep at the window of my prayers
I saw my tent was an orchard
And I a cloud that poured down onto the wild wastes
A rain from the shadows

4

I painted in gestures
An orchard
I painted in phrases
A perfume
I wrote in the book of longing:
Every human being
Can bind in friendship
Water and fire
And create from the darkness the day.

Yahia al-Samawy
English translation by Eva Sallis

4

Third Trimester

At thirty two weeks she resembles
a giant melon, minus the barrow beneath.
Her tight belly is a map of silver rivulets.
Her legs splay out like an old dog's.
Hands on hips she waddles to the bathroom,
tackles the stairs with the gait of the aged.
She no longer attends family dinners
where svelte sisters-in-law offer advice.

Her inner furnace rages.
She seeks a bedroom, flicks off
her damp tent-dress and bra
to lie full frontal by a window.
Rising, she thinks of upturned beetles.
She snaps and naps at odd moments.
She hasn't seen her feet for weeks
and the mirror announces her navel has gone.

A pang makes her want to wind back time,
return to the store and tell them this body doesn't fit
but a stirring from inside her, and she strokes
the stretched orb as if it were an egg.
She whispers things to keep it warm.
With big stitches and determination, she knits
her first crooked bootee while she waits
for the flood that will split her like an autumn fruit.

Jude Aquilina

Lunch hour

I lunched today with a dove
in Whitmore Square
our conversation was leisurely
as we pecked the crumbs away
another presence in the
circle of our sharing
caught us unaware
you silently fletched
my spirit and riffled
through my soul content
preening my ruffled destiny
I did not see you leave.

Maeve Archibald

Water Flow—Haiku

Further from the shore
indigo darkens cobalt
grey turns silver.

The sheen of silver
newly polished by the moon
picks out the shore.

Water song gushes
eases around the corner
joins a new stream.

Looking for water
I found the source of self
and breached the wall.

Deep water image
reflects a dark shadow
mirror for today?

Maeve Archibald

Falling Man at nine forty one, Sept. Eleven.

I am the falling man. You must accept
at 240 kilometers an hour, I am poetic.
There are no systems carefully crafted
to catch me with a trade advertisement
or stop the broken continuity of my text.

You pretend you do not know me, linear
falling quietly through the photographic
frames and flowing quality of the words
in an unbroken, endless, ten second loop,
your conversations compressed now, held.

I have only your gaze and the cameras
to hold me. I am inverted—a pattern, half-
enfolded by light; half-embraced already
by shadow against the bar graph verticals
—collapsed temporal forms following me.

Slow me. Observe. I resolved to dance.
I am the falling man, upside down;
the rhythm of my lifted feet tap in time.
I accept my death almost nonchalantly.
You can see this is no rope I sway on.

For you below, who sit where I once sat
at a café table, also balancing dominoes
and discussing news from behind the stage
about rehearsals for another state of play,
look up. I am forever here, the falling man.

Henry Ashley-Brown

Recipe for . . .

How to overcome the Hell-king himself
armed with nothing but a well-used credit card
And a side-order of attitude:

First, make sure you change the music—
Go for maybe a country and western surfie feel
Decorate the skulls with tie-dye bandanas
Import some palm-trees—they seem to like the heat—
Organize a scratch game of cricket down over the killing-fields
But don't let Cerberus be wicket-keeper—he'll eat the ball.

We'll go crabbing in the Styx and surfing the Acheron
Set up a barbecue over the lava pits
—Get the lower demons to do the salad—
Put together a raffle in all the Hell circles
First prize: a weekend with Beelzebub,
Second prize two, with Mephisto thrown in
So let's pave the road with good intentions
And find work for idle hands and claws and fangs
Asbestos cladding over all of the Infernal City:

Hell has nothing on the suburbs!

Avalanche

On Semaphore Beach

Well, a watch or a ring if I'm lucky,
he says, but more often a coin,
perhaps a bottle-top.
So I join him for a yarn
as he crisscrosses the sand
with a metal detector.
He tells me about the Balkans,
the shimmering mountains,
the alignment of valleys
and the middling soil.
The past has set lines round his eyes,
rasped furrows on his brow.
As he works, a song wheezes away
from his chest at times.
His forebears would have bent to plow,
their yield a compensation,
but in his homeland now
a harvest of landmines,
the cropping out of a bomb.
We don't speak of the rewards
that could be reaped there—
a life saved or a limb.

The day winds down
and early evening falls gently
with a fortune in its arms,
the waves unfolding on a shore
where the gulls too are fossickers,
making the most of things.

Elaine Barker

Teacher

When did my mind
Venture first
Into Poetry?—
It was when I first read
Colin Thiele's
The Mushroomer:

Which begins
(If my memory serves):

'Over the brow of the hill
The mushroomer, walking,
Felt the cry of lost
Lambs in his ears . . .'

And it goes on
To speak of how
'He threw away his bucket,
His wife,
And ten years' lamplight
And clutched at himself again.'

I haven't read it in 40+ years,
So Pardon me if my quote is less than perfect,
But the Poem itself
Is.

Yesterday we lost
Steve Irwin
And Colin Thiele
Both.
Both of them Great Australians,
Great Conservationists,
And beyond all,
Great Teachers.

Steve Irwin I never met
But Colin Thiele was my Lecturer in English,
And my Tutor in English
My Teacher for a year.

's funny you know
But just a week ago today I was at Clare,
Just me and Dog Bunsen,
Watching wild Kangaroos in the Wilderness;
Those very words of Thiele's on my mind,
As I too
Clutched at myself again.

I loved his writing.
He read aloud the best of anyone I ever met.
He changed my life
(And for the better too).
But now, as these things do,
It ends in tears.

Thank you Mr Thiele.

Bruce Bilney

Illusions

Looking back across the bay—water, hills
and sky are of a piece, fused in sheer light,
the air bright, magnetized by stones;
granite sings. Boats rock, one of the gentlest
things on earth. Beyond the causeway
the ocean swells, seagulls ride the waves.
I watch a vessel heading out to sea,
old memories bob up and down like buoys.

A fisherman your shape and size walks
towards me. The light tampers with time;
the illusion passes. Strange to miss
you now as if the untold years were dreams,
no more than the sunlight playing tricks
on the surface of the wind-blown sea.

Karen Blaylock

The Bather

The old woman was chopping banana stalks.
Fodder for her two cows.
She motioned me past,
over the muddy embankment to the river.

His nakedness
as he stood in the shallows
took me by surprise.
The eroticism of smooth brown skin
glistening with water.

He was mango and crème brûlée.
He was fine as spun sugar.
He was Siva.
I turned away from his sweetness

before he turned and saw me.
Re-emerged by the ruminating cows.
The old woman looked up from her chopping.
Her smile was knowing.

Mary Bradley

Should we go nuclear?

It's my year ten class.
The topic of their debate is 'Should we go nuclear?'
I inform them of the Howard government think tank of economists,
     physicists and scientists.
I wonder which way they will vote.
We have watched the video Chernobyl Heart;
the babies in orphanages with their brains separate from their bodies
while others sprout tumours bigger than soccer balls.
We read Dr. Tim Flannery's article on global warming.
Anthony reels off all the facts off the Internet;
he's done his homework.
Facts like Australia has the highest rate of greenhouse gasses in the world.
We look at renewable energy:
wind farms seem like an option
except there hasn't been much wind lately.
Solar power is a good idea, but then you need a new roof.
I point out the irony if our uranium from Roxby makes weapons to be used
     against us.
Perhaps the S.R.C. should raise money to build nuclear fall-out shelters.
The intellectually-disabled girl, Alicia, raises her hand to resolve the issue.
'Miss, don't worry about the radiation. The bird 'flu is coming.'

Kate Bristow

Radiotherapy

Dear John,
Been talking to Beth and Suzie
in Germany.
Maddie 'talked' too.
So did the little heart patient
from Ukraine
climbing dangerously in the background.

Here,
the crescent moon
sank through the almond tree
west of The Sisters and Olde Baron.
No doubt his red eye
featured in your Mustang navigation.
Pity your last flight
was such a spectacular disaster.
Not every pilot tips over a patrol dozer
with his Mustang.
At least it spared you
from Hiroshima's lingering radiation.
Your young brother was not so lucky.
He told me a bit
one long trucky trip to Victoria Market.
Wouldn't be many of them left:
the Occupation Forces overdosed in Hiroshima,
or the radiation guinea pigs
of Monte Bello and Emu Fields.
Your youngest sister outlived you slightly,
stricken with the congenital big C.
I'm the next test case.
I'll be radiant
after five days a week for seven and a half weeks.
At least I won't be vapourised
like Hiroshima's 'disappeared'.
Pinochet's thugs
could have learnt something from Hiroshima.
Unlike Angus, they missed the enlightenment.

Brian J. Brock

Visions on the Glenelg Tram

I saw robert dessaix
on the 1929 glenelg tram
escaping the writers' week crowd
he sat alone and unknown

I read moby dick
until the curved wooden ceiling
resembled neruda's residence at isla negra
built like a boat for the unmovable captain

forgetting my melville one morning
I was lost at sea amidst the creaking timber

I read don quixote
and the passing trams
were gallant knights engaged in battle
but my work was done

and the driver
framed in the light of the cabin window
reminds me each evening
of van gogh's postman
only clean shaven

and I did see patrick white
on the priority seats for the aged

and as for proust
his long sentences need rails

and neale
we read aloud your introduction
to shanghai journal
and it was as though you'd never died

Steve Brock

Having a Bit of Mum in Me

My mother is taking over my face.
It began with my body
my attitude, my stance.

Photographs betray her:
head thrown back in laughter,
or standing by a tree
watching her youngest
scoop tadpoles from a puddle.
I know it isn't me
because I'm in the puddle.

'Got a bit of Mum in you'
said my brother last time.
I really can't ignore it now
with one eye on the mirror
and the other on the clock.

Belinda Broughton

Between Stars and Trees

Tonight the stars have assembled on one plane
about two miles up.
Science can't convince me otherwise,
not tonight.
Tonight the trees have a tall black presence
and the space between the stars and them
is distinct and full of something—
more than air.
Perhaps it's our loved ones (living and dead)
or our love like beauty
or maybe when the heart is full like this
overflowing with the beauty of it,
maybe the feeling expands above the trees
ringing.
I'm sure if you put your head up there
you'd hear it.
In any case the trees are shaking their ears
and even though my warm blood
urges me inside, I won't go yet.
I'll lie here while these sacred trees
quietly shudder
turning the stars off and on
with their shaking.

Belinda Broughton

And Those Who Laboured

Dusk,
A Chinese city in the South.
The day's work ended
And those who laboured
Must now eat.

A restaurant
On the street,
Still empty,
The sun not yet down.

A cage
Hangs by the door,
A civet
In the cage,
Quivering nose,
Delicate, fingered paws
Gripping the bars.

A pet? In China, no.
This is a country
With customs different
In many ways
Not least, the culinary.

The evening passes.
In the hotel bar,
A resolution:
Dollars
For the civet's life,
The crazy *kwailo*
Will set his food free.

Out of the hotel
Now hurrying
Through the wet streets.

The restaurant,
Closed,
A cage,
Hangs by the door,
Empty
As the plates
Stacked ready
For the next day's meal.

John Brydon

A post modern appreciation of the male–female relationship paradigm

In former times
We all
Had sex,
But now
Make do
With gender.

John Brydon

Combo Waterhole

We were travellers passing through,
Tired and silent beside Combo Waterhole[1].
Dirty waters and dying coolabahs
Long past romance, the heart a shrunken thing,
A cracked creek and words emptied of meaning,
Carefully selected for loss.

Now beside the long road, dark birds extend
Claws and beaks. Undertakers with intimate business.
Here are the new milestones.
Bags of bones hunched in final prayer
God's perfect gift to this land, paws offered,
Then wasted in the silent rush.

How did we get here?
Redemption is a long road.
The bare trees frozen in a motion of escape
Life is death where sheep the colour of spinifex
Stand motionless, bowed on bald plains.
Under a sky, cruel blue, born of the Christmas child[2].
I dream of *mihirungs*[3], ancient thunder of the plains,
And of kindness as a gentle rain.

Anne Chappel

1 Combo Waterhole is the billabong where the swagman came to camp
   in Banjo Paterson's popular folk song, *Waltzing Matilda*
2 The Christmas Child—El Niño
3 Mihirungs—Aboriginal word now in use for the extinct giant birds
   that once flourished in ancient Australia

Spring Fever

No, Your Honor, my childhood was perfectly normal,
I never witnessed anything unspeakable,
Nor did anything unspeakable happen to me (as it does to youngsters
    of today):
The kids next door were pretty well kept in line by their parents: and
I was not bullied at school. My parents saw to it that I was fairly good,
Attended school regularly—did my homework.

Yes, I have a good ordinary job,
So there is nothing to account for it really.

And I do not know,
Nor can I account for the fact,

That, towards the end of August,
When the streets were still shiny,
Black, and chill,
I went out very early one morning

and deliberately let the air out of all my neighbours' tyres;

I opened all the garden gates right down the road, letting the dogs out:

I opened the cages of the birds, lonely cockies and budgies;

And even the pens of miserable chooks confined in viewless
    back yards.

And then I looked up at the clouds scattered across the sky,
slowly blushing to pink, bits of sparkly white,
and ran down to the beach and far along the glistening sands,

Screaming.

'Screaming maniacally'
the witnesses report:

and all the dogs running after me,
yapping like crazy, leaping,
long thin licorice shadows twisting joyously, independently . . .

Your Honor, I do not know why I did these things:
Only that I did them:

And I feel glad.

Betty Collins

Curve

of wild oat stalks
graceful in the breeze
husks delicately lit
after the fall of seed.
Fragile, these wild beauties.

Curve of eucalyptus bough
strong but brittle
in searing heat.
On the road,
Wimmera summer.

Dawn Colsey

The visit

We have had some unexpected visitors of late—
on the bird feeders flashes of red and green
announce the arrival of the greedy lorikeets
profligate with the seeds
which fall unheeded to the earth below.
Greenish-brown duck-billed visitors
waddle up the backyard or fly in
from the murmurous creek,
sometimes two, sometimes only one
as if to reconnoitre the territory for the other.
Spilt seed is the gourmet delight
with torn bread on the side
if we are quick enough.
They are shy and don't stay long,
just long enough to leave their calling cards in the grass,
the green, green grass.

Sue Cook

Camooweal Sunday

Still as desert places
the People sit in red dust
circle their fire
speak words from the Dreaming
ignore me
know I have not breathed their smoke,
for my history is measured in life spans
the Land only rock and earth
never to be in my blood.

Like cinders from wildfire
black kites swirl overhead,
incise their ancient patterns
on the white air.

David Cookson

Genes

As a child, I thought my Grandmother unique
eccentric to some, exotic as the parrots she kept
an Aladdin's Cave of knick-knacks jumbled on walls
always treats of baked biscuits, lollies from a jar.

From the dark haired, clear skinned bias
of endless youth, came teenage judgement.
Saw Grandmother's slow shuffle, soft slippers
worn year round, their heels crushed inwards
Vowed I wouldn't be like that.

Heard Grandmother with her sisters
share the world's biggest joke,
like farm house chooks, all a-cackle together
Swore I wouldn't sound like that.

Saw Grandmother, Aunties, a roly-poly army,
crimson, orange, purple patterned pinnies
that covered lumpy breasts, non-existent waists
Promised I wouldn't let that happen to me.

Caught just a glimpse of brown eyes
that crinkled at the slightest excuse
almost vanished into a street map of laugh lines
Dreaded the thought that could happen to me.

Touched that Mother Christmas hair
heard her sisters envy the silver-white mane
my Grandmother brushed till it sparkled
Hoped that wouldn't happen to me.

I can imagine my Grandmother,
that fountainhead of our gene pool
and hear her loud belly laugh.

Veronica Cookson

singer

There's true beauty
in the way
you don't hit the note
the way you float
somewhere close by
looking behind
your closed eyes
for the place to stop
the spot to land
the perfect landing place
and touch down
perfectly
off centre

Judy Dally

minda trees

sometimes
the sun shines
between
those crooked trees
and the shadows
they make
are both
straight.

Judy Dally

conductor

climb
onto the note
I'll give you
a hand-up

can you feel
the direction of the wind
or find
the next foothold?

I will
call down to you
with instructions
conduct you
to the right spot
at the right time

eventually
you will
see the view

Judy Dally

sometimes

sometimes
it's cold
in these old rooms

sometimes
you are so together
you don't need me

sometimes
you excel
without help

sometimes
all I can do
for you
is the dishes

Judy Dally

Ten freshly painted toenails

I found that part of my life today
you know
the one that's been missing
somewhere between
small snotty noses
and someone else's stress
Well I found it today
nestled between
a pot of tea
ten freshly painted toenails
and a set of lunchtime dishes
For the first time
in all of this
half gone year
my life became
how I remember it.

Jo Dekok

birdsong

i sit with birdsong in my ear
and my world dancing
   and contemplate emergence

i take this filter and overlay today
and see this blue-sky off
to hold that cloud still with my eye
to contain this gaseous blanket in my hands
   and consider resolution a lost, youthful art

we turn regardless
cheap gimbles squeaking now and then
my voice in friction wrought
my bearings weak
my direction nought
my aim to seek
to be the meek, the ringing squeak
the willing wheeling written speak
the bird the ear the cloud the eye
the air the hand the blue the sky
the art the dance the world and I

rdekok

When the heart stops

'When the heart stops' . . . you say . . .
your mouth is always dry, eyes closed,
you speak with difficulty.
'you think it is when the heart stops,
when the heart . . . stops.'
'Dying is a process.'

I know you feel your body checking out,
asking sometimes 'is it day or night?'
And I wait the unwinding of your words,
the release of your final Zarathustra.

You tell me your heart feels
like a tiny bird, I see it
caught by a thread around one foot,
ready to fly.

'When the heart stops' . . .
your pulse is racing,
and my heart is tearing open,
as I feel your life-time coalescing.

There is nothing that you might not do
in these moments. You
talk of stopping wars.
'Why are we still fighting?'
while your inner battle is
a firestorm in each cell,
each squabbling its separate deprivations.

Your mind running out of time,
still hunting for that 'All Thing' of thought,
the final solution.
We sit together, waiting
for your heart to choose its moment.

Jo Dey

The Voice

I have fallen in love with a voice.
I have fallen with head over heels.
Can't say why—love's not based on choice.
Like magnetic force, you can't see how it pulls,
But you certainly know how it feels.

There are others with velvet timbre
Just as likely to enthral.
And I've fallen before, more times than I care to remember,
So perhaps I too easily fall.

But I've never felt my heart so melt
Nor was I stirred so deep within
Until this funny Valentine voice
Got right under my skin.

The voice lives what it sings, seems sincere,
As if confessing truth in conversation
When relaxed with nearest and dear,
Free from all affectation.

O Rolls Royce vehicle for romantic ballads,
Interpreter of dreams, and stories too,
You've set the standard for all song-book standards
And I only have ears for you.

Such a sweet and tender trap!
Dedicated to love, forever homeward it calls.
But delinquent disgruntlement lurks in its sap,
Loading the words with emotional cannonballs.

It bothers and bewilders as much as it can bewitch and beguile.
And, as expressive as a failed lover with an FBI file,
It threatens the world, Mafia-style.

I'm sorry to be bending your ears.
But this torch that I've found has gotta be drowned
Or it may soon explode.
So: just one more stanza for my therapy
And one more for the road.

You're as soothing as the warm, summer wind
Gently tintinnabulating chimes,
As devout as David's harp would be
If plucked in modern times.

As serene as a chant by choir
Haunting medieval Chartres . . .
Oh, stop, you fool, before this praise gets any higher
Lest I go and spoil it all by saying something stupid
Like
I love Frank Sinatra.

Kalicharan Nigel Dey

Leavings

Lurking in gutters
along roads, footpaths
lying on green carpets
feigning inertia
they wait in ambush
—Autumn's fallen
waiting for sounds
of tyres on tarmac
heralding swift chance
for a final flutter.
Curved ears to the ground
front lines scatter forward
raised in a skirmish
of whirling vortices
lifting to brief new life
tumbling, spinning
a high spiralled fling
subsiding to
defiant assault
scratching, scuttling
like dogs worrying
at pedalling feet.

One remains aloft
pressed by the wind on
four-wheeled aerial spike
riding pennant-like
imaging former splendour
flagging last colours.

Genevieve Grace Drew

A Ghazal: Whale song

Breaching, the whale shines against the setting sun,
her song, deep and lost within the setting sun.

There is a longing that hungry pulls against
the tide of the setting sun.

It is never enough to paint a Kabuki mask
on a face that smiling shines like the setting sun.

He spoke of torturous journeys of love
on ancient roads abandoned by the setting sun.

You escaped on the wind in a wild sky
as she wept, blinded by the setting sun.

The black crow in raucous triumph glistens
in its flight into the setting sun.

I lie between the shimmering barley,
my flesh, warm and hungry beneath the setting sun.

Tess Driver

Julie

Week after week
In the old Thursday night venue
At the Union Hotel,
She enticed me to dance
To Sympathy Orchestra's
Strange time signatures.
15/8, 13/8, 7/4, 5/4, 6/4 . . .
Eventually I got the hang of them,
And now,
Even the aches and pains next day
Have gone away.
Perhaps I'm not as old as I thought . . .
Must change my age by deed poll
Before she asks me how old I really am.

Garth Dutton

Becoming

They were flares

They were flames

They were flares
Of pollen and scent

They were flames
Of lichen and salt

They were flares
Of pollen and scent
Soaring on the cliff

They were flames
Of lichen and salt
Roaring on the coast

She was

She was the trees

She was the trees
The rocks

Peter Eason

The forensic science of grief

You breathed your last breath from the air
in this room;
that threadbare Persian carpet
holds flakes from your skin;
hairs from your head
corkscrew the dented cushions
scattered and idly waiting on the sofa;
bed linen scented with your sweat
the goose-down doona that stole
your last warmth;
sleep spit and tears
human moisture that permeates
the acrylic layers of your pillow;
an eyebrow hair wedged in the tweezers;
a clipped nail that flew off
somewhere out of sight;
that new toothbrush used only once;
your flannel and towel still drying out;
the wet press footprint on the bathroom mat;
the talcum powdered slippers
abandoned under the brass bed.
Each moment of everyday
we shed ourselves
shed dead cells and renew—
a cycle of shedding
until the last
shedding of ourselves.

M.L. Emmett

Crow on the Cross

from the steeple cross
I see the glossed white tin
of your bridal car approaching—
I adjust tail feathers the lustre of coal
a porcelain sheen turns on my wings
deep as black water

I alight from the spire in a lazy arc
step into church with my coat ablaze—
was there ever as sleek a groom?
was there ever a sharper foil for a bride
than this lit darkness
this brilliance I am?

my beak is full of spells
a gush of wedding song
I will sing the fractured axis
I will sing the ghost of longing
I will sing the wild tilt of unearthed things
and pour us back into the sky—
we will fly
bird and bride
and all the angled winds
a riff on the bible of flight

see
your plumage already begins to grow
come with me
leave your long white car
leave your grieving family—
the mouth of death won't have us yet
let them look for us in skies and trees
we will look back from the little cross
we will peer through the stained glass
and sing our inelegant songs
the hymns to loss and faith
the long wet light of winter on us

Steve Evans

Bridges

Bridges cross from one place to another:
Right Bank to Left Bank of the Seine
over a low arched bridge of stone;

over the green canal at Annecy
flowing out of the mountain-rimmed lake
past bridges with flower baskets by canals,
old buildings with their feet in water;

Bridge of Sighs and many other bridges
over canals where gondolas ply
and pink stucco houses flake away
as the sea rises;

bridge of latticed steel over the harbour
in Sydney where the hills come down
to the blue water, and somewhere remembered
are the echoes of Bennelong and the dispossessed,
submarines sharks and yacht races
white and coloured sails
billowing over the riffled water.

But there was no bridge
over the Jordan in the days of Joshua
whether the city of Jericho stood or not,
so between here and what is to come
there is no bridge but that which faith constructs.

Margaret Fensom

Caravan park theory

Do not air dirty laundry
On the communal clothesline
warns a sign on the ablution block.
I look over at white sheets waving in the wind,
shake the sand from my board shorts
and mark with pegs a site of resistance.
Trying to evade surveillance,
I walk along the side streets,
past begging seagulls and onsite vans
flanked with crates of empty beer bottles.
Radios announce the soundtrack of summer
will once again be 'classic rock'.
But here, there's the rhythm and melody
of raised voices, slamming aluminium doors
and thongs slapping concrete.

A crowd gathers within a city
of silver-domed tents.
Their efficient use of space,
their ordered arrangements of lines
while queuing for food: faultless.
From the outskirts, they stare suspiciously
at my shanty tent—my Kmart holiday.

After unwinding their second home, a family settles in
to a routine. Mum reads an erotic short story
in a magazine. Dad lies on a deck chair, day dreaming
about licking beer-flavoured ice cream
from his favourite swimsuit model's breasts.
Under pine trees, kids run across scattered needles
and through sprinklers, screaming
and soaking themselves in treated water.
At the van, Mum offers a towel,
Dad sends them to the kiosk for ice cream.
The nuclear family exploded long ago,
but its fragments are found
in caravan parks every summer.

The long afternoon
is a slow-cooking casserole—
all gristle and juice.
Bodies that glisten with sunscreen
move in and out of water as slow as the tide,
leaving only when the sun ushers them out.
The arrival of darkness
is signalled by the sizzle of barbecues
and mozzie zappers frying meat.
As voices float in the breeze,
the park finds its nightly rhythm
in the muffled crash and fizz
of waves, of bodies
curling under sheets.

Cameron Fuller

The design of status

it's a pair of branded sport shoes
made in a sweat shop
for two dollars
bought for two hundred
and worn with a confidence
that filters out the noise
of a thousand sewing machines
pounding on your conscience

Cameron Fuller

Sonnet
(Writers' Week in Adelaide 2006)

I am sitting in different shadows. Chairs are the roots of trees,
the white tents a nest of words and creation.
I am listening to the sound and face of vowels.
Names and authors are beings of the image world.

Stories of lands, struggles, deaths,
beauty and ugliness an equal part of the journey.
Foreign sounds are rare birds under native trees.
A kookaburra sings to the wind and the heat of the evening.
Yahia al-Samawy reads his poem in Arabic:
'Leave my country—
The helmet of occupiers can never be a pigeon's nest.'

I am listening to the rhythm of hearts next to a tree
I am listening to Robert Fisk's flesh, wounded lines,
Baghdad and Gaza his home, ancient cities
without rivers, only dried dreams of the oppressors.

Juan Garrido-Salgado

Adelaide in Autumn

It is the month of May
and the plane trees in North Terrace
are singing us into winter
with notes left over from summer.
One by one they drop their leaves,
words that scuttle along the path,
pile up like pages from the past
to tell us tales of those whose plaques
we walk upon each day.

In their own way
these plain and unassuming trees
could stand as living memorials
to life and death and then re-birth
the everlasting cycle
that adds depth
to the compost of our history
all neatly packaged in one great boulevard,
the backbone of this city.

Jill Gloyne

Poets on Popeye

the peal of cathedral bells
shivers blossoms

and echoes across the white shell
of the theatre

to the river
a curling silver serpent

alive with rowing eights
and the blue and white Popeye

as it chugs to the weir past water reeds
where birds nest in the safety of dusk

laughing poets recline
and listen to poetry that flows

as gently as the Torrens itself
they lean over the side of the boat

trail fingers at gliding black swans
who communicate their delight

in guttural sounds of pleasure
as they majestically swim alongside

it is hard to choose
whether to listen to the reader

or the swans

Jill Gower

Semaphore

under the overcast
grey as flannels

were worn wool & rough
from a past

of hats tilted
rogues at the top

of the street
& the blue

of Gulf water
from the ferris

wheel's night
sky turning

around & around
inside of us

rory harris

mother

& a daughter
throws flowers

from the end
of the jetty

a string
of grand daughters, sons

a son in law
mid morning Sunday

water scrunches
as a face would

just before the tears

rory harris

Unity—the Design

Turn a circle on its side;
Stretch a line around the Earth.
Each becomes the other then—
Fecund signs for Sex and Birth.

The straight line male, yet female too,
The circle woman—also man;
Comprehended, line in circle
Since the flow of Time began . . .

Thus it's been and thus will always—
None can say if curve or line
Is worse or better in its purpose,
For both reflect the Great Design.

Geoff Hastwell

Tempo

Masts metronome
the beacon blinks in double time
the pianist doesn't bother . . .
Waiters at the marina café
outcount the diners
two to one
like the beacon behind the masts.

One drink and I am sleepy
like the town
lullabied
by the quiet guitar
on the background tape.
The unhurried pianist
helps me translate
a printed napkin.

All's well . . .
until an orange cloud
and a delayed crescendo
rip open a tourist bus
and the new world
terrorizes
our collective dreams.

Roger Higgins

Composing music

rain petalled
      across the garden

as she stared at the music
      that trickled down
           the window-pane of her senses

violin arpeggios glistened
      in the silence

as flowers wept

Sally Ann Hunter

Peace exists

Today I adopted
an abandoned tyre,
rolled it back
along the creek,
and tomorrow
I will paint it
brilliant blue,
plant strawberries
inside, and watch
life grow anew.

Because peace exists . . .
. . . waiting to be found.

Indigo

Retroactive

I won't stand for mediocrity
I've been lying with it too long.
I'm living in the moment—
this one isn't priceless, or cheap.

I am that bug caught between
a green juice glass
and yesterday's news
waiting feverishly to be let outside.

Indigo

Twice Upon a Time

Midnight has come and gone.
Glass slippers
long since kicked aside.
Disenchanted Cinderellas
recall age-old fairytales
that promise a future
of perpetual elation.
Recall handsome amphibians, who—
in the cold light of day—
turned out to be toads or crocs.

Wonder why they didn't
take advice from Red's old granny.
She knows a wolf when she sees one—
knows him inside out.
That handsome *is*, as handsome does.
That a regular frog
who'll hang out the washing
and cook up a stirfry
is worth two posers in the pond.

Shirley Ireland

Obituary

He lived in the Trope-ical Zoo.
Risk was mother's milk to him.
He thrived on curds of cliché
and carried a sawn-off simile under his shirt.

Bit of a card, a blokey joker,
he'd hit a hyperbole broadside and T-bone himself,
but he always bounced back.

He was a folk anthology for the risk-averse,
for voyeurs, toyers, second-hand eyes,
small-screen Pajero heroes,
his pages clamped with an alligator clip.

His fans sprayed him with mixed metaphors.
Safe from the critics' stingray barbs,
he was struck by the irony of life.

He lies in Australia's Poetry Zoo,
buried beneath the Thesaurus,
his headstone the Macquarie Dictionary
open at 'crikey'.

Patricia Irvine

Snake

I am the broken branch that breathes,
the dancer's copper bracelet,
the live mathematics of sine and coil and torus,
rope and whip made flesh,
the secret vine that craves the sun,
the winding track through seadunes
of spinifex and marram.
I am words sorted, magicked into shape,
ordered and shuffled at the speed of breath
as you sit writing me.
Respect me, let me be. I keep
the gate of paradise.

Patricia Irvine

Lonely nest

The empty nest syndrome with a twist
as it was me who was turfed out,
a relationship that soured
and the last child leaving home
I was on my own elsewhere
disorientated, upset
a freedom not sought.

Didn't have to be available at school home time
or with a meal ready at tea time
or back at a decent hour for the baby-sitter
could stay out all night
all week—if I wanted.

But this was my home
and I could stay in as much as I wanted,
not being disturbed by rowdy late home teenagers
(let's continue our party in the kitchen)
war movies on stereo TV
that night-owl unable to keep decent hours
or waiting for the last person in the household to arrive home.

It was this freedom that upset me most
I guess it was the caring
always a family to fret about
all flying back to the nest at night
but I wasn't there any more.

Just one to cook for
watch my favourite shows
listen to music, read
nobody else to consider
but as I settle down for the night
now able to tolerate a solitary bed
something undone, missing still—
the doors are locked, what else?
Waiting for the family to come home
years on, still the feeling of anticipation
waiting, ever waiting
for the family to come home.

Rosemary Jaensch

A view of the Hills

Look back on the hills you walked on
and they're somewhere you've never been.
There's a view of the Hills through the window
here at the cardiac centre where my wife
is in for a scan. I sit, an old man alone
along with the others who wait, all of us
stony and silent, stiffly ignoring each other
except for one woman in sexy
stiletto-heeled boots who stands gazing out
of the window. My eyes flutter idly
between her and the softly traced line
of sun-bleached grass and dusky woodland—
no sight at this distance of any
landmark I know or road I have travelled
and it strikes me—if there's a point
to the journey it has to be somewhere between
a past I remember in patches
and a future where I'll never arrive
in a place such as this where life
thins out to a line on a screen.

Rob Johnson

A villanelle for today

How suitable this form for laissez-faire
Employers freed to do now as they please.
No pastoral pleasures for the workers there.

This French term—all workers should beware—
Those with power can bring them to their knees.
How suitable this form for laissez-faire.

No out of bounds, no thought outside the square
No extra payments and no more penalties
No pastoral pleasures for the workers there.

Managers can rule, reject the need to care
Who dare question when a wage might freeze?
How suitable this form for laissez-faire.

Safe behind new laws, away from the glare
Of frightened mortgagers, anxious families.
No pastoral pleasures for the workers there.

With less than a hundred, free to be unfair,
Dismiss at will, ignore convention's niceties.
How suitable this form for laissez-faire—
No pastoral pleasures for the workers there.

Erica Jolly

Mutton dressed as lamb

It was a fear that stalked my mother.
Lose the frills?
Colour too bright?
Hem too high?
Too much black?
Really, finally, just too old
for this year's look?
Then there was the other, equal dread.
A bit matronly maybe?
Colour too drab?
Hem too low?
Too much of the lavender and pearls thing?
Is it stylishly classic
or just plain dowdy?
I had little patience with it.
I'll tell you, I'd promise.
Trust me.
I wouldn't lie.
It's fabulous.
Now I detect
the same tentacles of doubt.
The eyes staring back at me
in the dressing room mirror
are unsure
anxious.
I've seen them before.
Will I look a fool?
Will people snigger?
And my daughter sighs,
and replies,
with uncomplaining fortitude.
It's fabulous, trust me.

Cheryl Jordan

Coming up for air

amniotic sac
full flowing forward
toward parting of waters
holding in free fall
a foetal form, growing repletion
for first frontal feeling
of oxygen-aerated molecules,
offering first function,
                                        life-force!

greeting!
joyful, waiting world . . .
livve now,
alive? now livve
long enough
to bear
sad aches
of live reality
of learned reality
of engineered reality
of real reality
of news-noise reality
silent movie, reel-three-reality
            cascades now

into sentry-century
with
            Sound! Light! Picture!
Gutsy,
Organismic Roar————
Love unconditional bears all . . .
bares all in flush of
naked berth;
Goodwill to all the child;
Think-peace on earth . . . . . .

Khail Jureidini

Poets Anonymous

It's been five days since I've touched a poem.
A year ago, I was a thirty-poem-a-day man,
then it all came crashing down . . .

When my wife kicked through the dunes of unpublished drafts
and bookmarked anthologies and coffee-stained collections
to drag her suitcases across the house and out the door,
when I heard the car back down the drive, then fade away,
I went to the bar to pull myself together with a swig of
   'Poet's Corner' shiraz,
and finally saw the dust and spider webs behind the façade of my life—
—nice imagery that . . . *that* . . . rhymes with *cul de sac*
           the bungee-jumping *cat*
           slipped the loop, went *splat* . . .

sorry . . . old habits, you know . . .
As I was saying, after she and the kids walked out
I just went mad—I bashed a hole in the wall
with a first edition hard-back of Blake's complete works,
read Keats' 'Ode to Melancholy' eighteen times straight,
no chaser, then demolished all twelve books of 'Paradise Lost',
then passed out halfway through writing a Sonnet denouncing women,
prose writers, the Arts Council, and a stubborn muse . . .

When I came to, a rat was chewing on Friendly Street thirteen
-on the page featuring my first ever published poem in fact-
my tongue was coated with bits of onomatopoeia and half-rhyme,
my head felt like Auden's arse, the electricity had been cut off
and divorce papers had been shoved under the front door.

It started so innocently. I was in control.
Just a quick Villanelle before breakfast. One Emily Dickinson
and half a Lydia Simkus after lunch, and for a nightcap a quick Haiku of
   my own
(only a first draft mind you)
I was in control. OK, so a book of 'The Prelude' got me through to
   morning tea
and the biscuits and the coffee quickly gave way to the composition
of one, then two, then five poems
washed down with a *lot* of polish
—I was in control,
even if I was arm-wrestling with rhymes
and scanning dark devoursome lines

at the same time as bracket-my-God-bracket
I was (God!) talking to my wife and kids . . .

I should have tweaked when Sylvia, my youngest, ran away from
    pre-school
and hid in an oven in Harvey Norman's for six hours before she
    was spotted
—her letter (in rhyming couplets) told me I never listened to anything she
    or her mum said
unless it was a figure of speech which I immediately changed
into an extended metaphor. She said all I cared about was
Dawe's irony and Dickinson's delicacy of tone and Plath's cruelty to bees
and Lily Brett's obsession with Poland
and that I was becoming seriously weird gross
embarrassing and boring.

I should have heard the alarm bells . . . five of them, coldly ringing
    out . . . sorry!
I'm in control . . . see the dream, feel the dream, plan the . . .
I am prosaic. I am invincible.

But back then I only thought I was in control . . .
I should have *known*
In the hollow of my *bones*
. . . sorry, sorry . . .
Then it happened . . . tragedy walloped me like the proverbial
    onomatopoeia. Walt, my
eldest, threw all the poetry books I'd given him into the combustion heater
    while I was out at a reading, and when I got in muttering some Heaney
    to myself he broke down in tears and told me what he'd done and said
    he hated me
and just to rub it in used a cliché instead of a fresh expression saying
'For the rest of my born days the only things I'm going to read are
    traffic signs,
computer icons, Christmas cards and Ralph.'
By this time my wife was threatening to call the police every time
    assonance,
conceit, iambic pentameter or sprung rhythm was used,
figuratively speaking, to pin her down . . . 'Post-Romantic harassment' she
    called it. And I realized I was out of control,
but I just couldn't control it. I was getting up in the night pretending to go
    to the toilet but actually dashing off at least three free-verse dramatic
    monologues on the toilet paper because the half-kilogram volume of
    Pound's complete works

that I hid in the cistern had been found and chucked out—
I had Charles Bukowski lines stuck to the bottom of the gin, whisky,
vodka and Kahlua bottles. I'd uncorked all of my red wine,
put a rolled-up Dylan Thomas poem into each bottle, then re-corked them.
The telephone book had epigrams written in invisible ink at the top of
    every page . . .
when my wife saw me holding the phonebook up to the light whenever
    I made a call
I said I was suffering from astigmatism.

Near the end, I had Byron on my walkman, a Braille copy of 'The Road
    Not Taken'
inside my shoe to get the cadence with every step,
another copy inside my sock in case my wife found the one in my shoe,
and a traditional Japanese haiku stuffed up each nostril
to get it straight into the bloodstream. I'd lost my job by then
because my work computer was full of poems, I answered the phone
    in verse,
dressed like Prufrock, and kept breaking into Geoff Goodfellow recitations
whenever I was telling clients why Semaphore was the perfect place to buy
    a house.
Which was ironic because by then I didn't have a house.
It was tough, huddling under a bridge or inside a skip
with nothing but a few metaphysical images to keep myself warm with
and simile-aversion therapy to look forward to the next day
and then the cold assonance bath

and just when I thought I was cured
I took a houseboat holiday on the Murray
and it started all over again, but worse . . .

So I've come along to poets' anonymous.
It's been five days since I wrote a poem
A week since I read one.
I admit, to all of you here,
That I'm a versaholic.
It started with my first nursery rhyme
and led me to all this shame
—I just want to be literal again.

Geoff Kemp

For my father

For my father's world was safer
Story-stitched
Adam and Eved
But
Birthy unpredictable feminine grotesque
It split open
As it often does
As pomegranates do.

Once he found one as a child
Split open by birds
Swinging from a shrub
Showing the shining seeds within
Dark as blood
Red as rubies
And at the foetal centre
A millipede curled
Up like a Darwinian fossil.

Women he found
Messy, unpredictable
Feeling-pitched
Cats, witch-like,
Trees made him sea-sick.

He dreamed of blind
Motorcyclists with no headlights
Ramming him at intersections.

He sat in his car in the snow
With the fuses pulled out
Trying to dream himself
Back to white.

For my father struggled with this world
Hated, controlled it
And us
Through the sermon
Wrote poems about shining pearls of
Wisdom awaiting
Discovery on unspoilt beaches.

For my father's
Final resort was
The act of labelling
The world with words;
The feverish application of
Post-it notes that,
Had we known it then,
Were
Little yellow life-buoys
For a drowning man.

Michael Kingsbury

The Port Noarlunga Hotel

The man in
the front bar

Has no entrances
or exits

Always sits on
the same stool

As if permanently
on tap

Long after the night
has broken through his eyes

He casts out his bric-a-brac
philosophies

To anybody who
is left

Only to reel in another beer
and then

Another
while his thoughts are tangled

Up in the barmaid's
fishnet stockings

Jules Leigh Koch

Train trip

I remember
a panoply of eventide dreaming
on the train home
a Friday night ritual.
As the train
sauntered into the station
I spotted the station master
and then
the name 'Riverton'
in big sombre black letters.

I remember
seeing my mother.
She was standing tall
a swaying tree
her hair
soft and silken
tied up in a perfect bun.
Brazen as Goldilocks
I skipped off the train
precarious moments
before it came to a grinding halt.

I remember
the bracing walk home
with my mother
past the line of shops
(Never anything I wanted to buy)
All the time
so happy
(I had my mother to myself)
for this everlasting golden moment.

Donna Kouis

Housing Estate in the Howard Era

Modular mansions in pastels and creams,
'Entertainment areas' designed
around wide-screen TVs.
The windows are huge
but the curtains are drawn—
Pragmatism won't see it is ideology.

Fat-arsed cars are the local gods,
and double garages their shrines.
Gardens shrunk to lozenges and tabs,
and narrow paths to the washing lines.
More bedrooms than people.
These structures agree:
'Don't relate to the street.
Everything's inside, and for me.'

Mike Ladd

The Legislative Assembly

I will say this again so you can hear.
I will say it again so that you can hear.
I am pleased to have the opportunity
to speak to the report—the report
by the Public Bodies Review Committee,
'Towards Better Performance Reporting.'

I congratulate the Review Committee
on the work it has done conducting
the workshops and compiling this report.
And I am pleased to have the opportunity
to speak to this report—this report
which provides the honourable members
here in the Legislative Assembly
with evidence that the government
is failing the people of this State.
The report shows that some ministers—
such as the Minister for Fair Trading
who is at the table—that these ministers
are interested only in theatrics.
I will say it again so that you can hear:
they are interested in mere theatrics
and they are not interested in delivering
services to the people of this State—. . .

I commend your ruling, Mr. Acting Speaker:
there is obviously no point of order here:
I am not attacking the Minister
I am talking about his committee's report,
a report making a number of assumptions,
making a number of incorrect assumptions
and a number of misleading assumptions
which I shall now run through here.
The Auditor-General has documented
in front of the budget committees
that Treasury is complicit, that Treasury
is complicit in failing the people—. . .

The Honourable Member may wish,
may wish to gag debate on the failure,
the failure of the government
to deliver basic services, to deliver—. . .

Thank you, Mr Acting Speaker
I am aware of Standing Order 67.
I am aware that Standing Order 67
warns against members repeating
repeating sentiments already expressed
at the risk that they may be ordered
to resume their seats on the ground
on the ground of repetition.
However, the Acting Speaker will be aware
that at the time he took the point of order
I was responding to an interjection—. . .

I appreciate your ruling, Mr Acting Speaker
and I advise I will present fresh argument
in dealing with this report here today,
this report that shows the failings
the consistent, habitual failings
of the government towards the people—. . .

Thank you Mr Acting Speaker
for advising me of your earlier ruling.
I will confine my remarks to the report
to the subject-matter of this report;
to avoid repetition, I am moving now
to a new part of my contribution.
I stated before that the Treasury
was complicit in allowing the failure—. . .

I thank you Mr Acting Speaker,
for your ruling on this matter
and I shall now resume my seat.

Stephen Lawrence

Walking

Step . . . by step . . . by step . . . by step
Slow . . . but it's progress.
Rain outside—rhythmic, driving,
placidly persistent.
It's my melody for
movement!

Lynx

Aunt Helene

I breathe in big, then push open
the gate to Aunt Helene's tatty square of garden.
It's been 4 years, we hug
She has the smell of smoke & sweet dog
as she talks her lips curl up
like crinkle cut cabbage with the politics
and that old South London accent,
but she is smiling almost innocently as Oscar does laps of the square,
takes me into the house, 'Come-on Oscar' she says

She makes macaroni cheese with over half gruyere 'my little luxury'
pours me a glass of wine, she doesn't drink anymore
while the food is cooking, she shows me round the walls
the collection of things & pictures from America
where her daughter is living, but I am watching her face

doesn't eat the seeds of tomatoes,
scrapes them out when she chops tabouleh
she doesn't say too much—except about her daughter

before eating we head out the back
smoking allows air out, lets her keep in
the grubby London secrets of her family
the hopes she had for her daughter
lost somewhere down Walworth lane
her grief about herself

two hours later, I hear her clump up the stairs
and climb into bed with the dog

*K*m Mann*

Pergolesi's Stabat Mater 1736

almost unbearably dramatic
after Fauré's requiem on the CD
this work by Pergolesi
from an earlier century
hits from the blind side
like the invention of emotion

no amount of silence
enough from the recording company
to justify this segue

after what had to be the last word
the perfectly pencilled ineffable blue
of Fauré's 'in paradisum'
this is a red crayon

a black cross in a stark field
with one woman weeping

pangs past consolation

and Pergolesi only lived to twenty-six
and knew that he was dying

in longer years he might have suppressed
or toned it all down as a sin of youth
too emphatic

but this has God's own urgency
for rest eternal granted unto
all and him and her and us
hopeless and tactless and operatic

more than fifty years before the Mozart
a hundred and fifty before the Verdi

David Mortimer

Reflection

I often think
why would the sun bother
getting into every puddle?
But it does

clearly and absolutely
bright after rain

At just the right angle

to persuade mathematicians
the world is real

David Mortimer

Flak Jacket

Politicians love returned soldiers
In theory

But in practice
Keep what distance they can

From people fully trained
To solve problems with guns

David Mortimer

Chinese Whispers

Time slips, en-roughs a slippered shod foot, stammers into fate,
a mined agricultural nightmare of fields ploughed
with the stone spittle of Chinese immigrants, thousands marching
north, way north of Adelaide.

Little bugga coolies with straw hats, pots & pans, hung from cut-cane
or fallen branch, jerky-leathered lean yellow-brown bodies
bearing on stick-insect shoulders; crucifixions bending under the weight
of home-grown haberdashery, handkerchief-tied food
for a thousand miles.

Spurred on the whisper of a wurlie forged by heinous hope,
blind desperation and cruel kites of optimism on ships from Darwin,
blown down with twisted time tooth-gapped sailors' rumour,
laughing, drunk on scurvy and drop-death breath,
the seamen mainline malignant half-truths, ruby-red rocks,
songlines of silver, gorges of gold, denizens of diamonds.

On gut feeling & grandfathers' knowing, they walk with these
Beelzebub-borne stories, fuel for hurry-hurry
& on reaching destination, slant eyes scan miles of plumb
pick-bombed holes, ant volcano-lipped red earth
whored limestone digs, scattered tools and scavenger
crow-cursed rocks, the Chinese whisper, drop their packs, set up camp.

Glen Murdoch

Threshold

These days, before I leave the nursing home
I call upon my father
to sit beside her bed, take her hand
and repeat his vows of sixty years ago
when he was a Clark Gable look-alike
in air-force uniform, cap askew
and she wore her hair like June Allyson
in The Glen Miller Story.
And in a few days or weeks or months
(she took her time back then
so perhaps she will again)
she'll look into the clear grey-green of his eyes
and realize the possibilities—
>   an eternity of encircled arms,
>   clouds of Palais Royal elegance,
>   moonlight serenading the night sky.

Allow him to carry her
across the threshold
one more time.

Louise Nicholas

Nevin Street, Hobart

This house is on the edge,
between the dark mass of bush,
thick as viscous oil at night
pouring down Mt Wellington's side.

Set against
the connection of a bitumen road,
so steep that even my little green car
pants for breath as we climb.

In the afternoon,
the mountain's presence burdens
this cottage with a deep cold,
that echoes within the marrow
of my human bones.

During the evening,
those from behind the dark
wall of trees
investigate my backyard.

Wallabies, possums leave grass-scented
droppings to step on,
but aren't seen, except for eyes
that reflect car headlights at night.

And the scuffling heard at 3am
from the roof,
reminding me that these visitors
are only an advance party,

ready to reclaim
this hillside from roads,
houses and the mystery
of street lamps.

Juliet Paine

Afternoon at Buongiorno's

* * *

Poetry with a capital P was drinking a latte
at Buongiorno's in Rundle Street
where cars and pedestrians
sweat a common urban cloud, a mist
like spray near waterfalls only thicker,
hardened by the heat
emanating from the bitumen below.
It's hot and perhaps a latte
is not the best drink for such weather,
so let's begin again.

* * *

Poetry with a capital P was drinking lemon,
lime and bitters at Buongiorno's in Rundle Street
when Mephistopheles appeared
dressed in a T-shirt which said, 'My brother
went to Romania and this is all he brought me.'
He looked good and had a new deal:
he was interested in migrant poets
from new zones of conflict because, as we know,
the Romanian revolution was sixteen years ago—
who would be interested to hear how scared I was then,
people need to know how scared other people are now.

So, like I said,
he sat down and asked me what I've been writing lately.
Well, I said, I'm interested more and more
in the lyrical stance of the ordinary,
in cadence and rhythm.
Bullshit, said Mephistopheles.
Poetry with a capital P sipped at her cold fizzy drink
and left the whole weight of the conversation
on Mephistopheles' shoulders—they were slender
but well-defined, manly yet beautifully shaped.
You still admire beauty
Wherever you see it, Mephistopheles smirked.

* * *

Take three: Poetry with a capital P
and Mephistopheles in a sweaty T-shirt
asked me to wear a Gretchen dress
while asking Gretchen questions—

do we have to write about politics
do we have to write about sex
do we all have to do it in a fixed form

and other such questions
that hissed on hitting the hot bitumen
swirled through the air like mad balloons
and unsettled the passers-by of that city afternoon.

* * *

People looked at each other on that afternoon at Buongiorno's
and shook their heads—
olives spelled elegant verses on pizzas,
cannelloni arranged themselves in stanzas,
there was a fresh metaphor in each foccacia
and drinks had layers upon layers.

Ioana Petrescu

The Old Airstrip

I found it by accident
flat concrete stretching out of sight,
three old air-raid shelters,
their curved roofs green with grass and weeds,
crouching in the shadow of trees.
Returned the next day,
for it was perfect—
straight and flat,
no cracks at all.

Like a lot of our things,
my skates had come from a catalogue,
not a shop:
their thin metal and plastic
didn't make the deep rumbling sound
that other girls' skates did,
but I did my best that day,
tried everything I knew,
took risks unheard of—
and the deserted shelters watched,
their broken doors ajar with wonder,
their camouflage of weeds and grass
as motionless as an audience caught
unaware.

Though I looked for it the next day,
and many other days,
I never found that old airstrip again,
with its perfect surface,
and the shelters from another time.
And though I tried,
I couldn't find that girl, either,
who skated like a star,
so smooth and sure.

Barbara Preston

Johnny's fireside chat—(how to boil Frosche.)

Menschen and Women of Australia
it is my solemn and unfortunate Duty
to inform you that, as of late last Nacht,
it has become Kristal Klar
a Putsch has been organized against Our Government.

Ein Mann of towel-headed Extraction
was caught on the grounds of Parliament Haus,
having reduced the foyer to ashes.

(I am also sorry to say the works of Pro Hart,
an Australian who I deeply Admire
were unrecoverable.)

Our highly efficient Polizeioffizierkorps caught him pretty Schnell
and he is now in Indefinite Detention,
as Prescribed by Section 1984 of the Anti-terrorism Act.

I appeal to all good Volk of Australia to keep Calm—
no need to go Overboard.
Stay in your Lebensraums—do not venture into the Strasse;
We are busy clearing it of Irresponsible Elements.

Check your fridge doors daily;
stay Achtung and Alarmed.

Please rest assured that we are in Complete Control of the Stadt.
My Cabinet is meeting tonight to draft new Verbotens
in order to deal with this Issue.

Alles is, as I have said, particularly Klar—
the vast international Konspiration
ıf Muⁿⁱⁱliⁿⁱⁱⁱⁱ ⁱ ⁱ Cⁱⁱⁱⁱⁱ ⁱⁱⁱ₍ Cⁱⁱⁱ ⁱⁱⁱⁱⁱ Tⁱⁱⁱⁱⁱⁱⁱⁱ,
is on the Move.
We must be Vigilant.

To this End,
rail trucks are being Prepared—
kindly donated by Patrick's Korporation
to ship Dissident Elements to offshore Locations
where their Influence on the Fatherland will be contained.
A final Pacific Solution is well in Hand.
As you know, and as I have said Before,
We will decide who Remains in this Country, and under what
    Circumstances.

You will be Pleased to Hear
our Doktors have Determined
a thorough program of Re-education, Cold Showers,
and a solid diet of Arbeit McFries
for these guests of the Stadt—
Café latte and chardonnay will be strictly forbidden.

Furthermore, it is clear from this Event,
that if you are not For Us, you are Against Us.
Therefore, all Small-minded Businesses,
as a display of National Loyalty in a Troubled Zeitgeist,
will install Flagpoles on their premises.
We also ask all Citizens to fly the Flag;
a Pole in every yard.

The Peril comes in many colours, meine freunden—
Yellow, Red and Green.
Help protect Australia from this Terrorismus—
every bit of information helps to keep Order.
With your help, and the new Diktats,
we will Ubercome,
and we will keep this Great Country of ours
free for a thousand Jahrs.

Gute nacht
And gute luck.

John Rice

True Love

I feel good
without your love
sorcerer's circles
around the heart
I have our harmony
and my own breath
and your touch
on body and soul
burning
I finally see
I am of the universe
and of myself
and then
maybe a little
of You

Alice Riedl

Doing something

Starting with the crisping drawers
I shave black edges off the cabbage;
just manage to save & use the celery
before it turns wet yellow straw.
To keep the last carrot, I lop off
the soft, thin edge of its wedge.
The only potato I can't countenance
is succulent into flower already.
It's all soup to me. Almost all.

All things ice come out for global warming.
Of course, nothing's used past its USE BY
even if it's the day before or the day.

I've demolished the cinnamon on jam on toast.
I'm working away at the nutmeg on icecream.
Could be thirty years old. The nutmeg.

Cooking salt is table salt to me.
The whole jar & I are slugging it out.
A pinch on this, a pinch on that
but not too much too soon or
my arteries will give out
before I'm through

finally doing something for The Third World.

Graham Rowlands

Long-suffering

I'm long-suffering
she says & she says
she's long-suffering
a few hours later &
only a few minutes
after that she says
she's long-suffering
& then after only
a minute or two
she says it again:
I'm long-suffering &
then again & again:
I'm long-suffering
I'm long-suffering &
I'm long-suffering too.

Graham Rowlands

Sonnet of the Fall

Apples are predictably sweet and sound,
plucked from espaliers wired on stone-wall rings,
but gnarly crabs wind-blown in riotous ground
give tart bounty to feed unfettered things.

Nourish passion that is sensual and bright,
for lust is leavened by care and duty.
Relish the garden of earthly delight,
it grafts the soul with heartbreaking beauty.

Keeper purse your mouth on the crab that's sour,
remember tender stems stand little chance;
if you frost the buds before the flower,
there will be no joy in the harvest dance.

Exquisite is the taste of sweet and sour,
I would know it all by the final hour.

c m runnel

A Race of his Own

A five year-old running his first race on sports day
ablaze in royal blue T-shirt and shorts, sunhat bobbling,
is herded into a ragged line; he needs manoeuvring,
his eyes not focused, radiating wonder—
he's alone in a stadium as big as the world,
and the crowd roaring. They're off
to a staggered take-off that he misses
but the teacher pushes him into the track.
A sideways swing to his body hampers his action;
at last he's there—at the finishing line.
The others have already straggled across the field
into the hugs of mums and dads.

I won, I won, he shouts.
Some heads turn surprised, and even
more beautiful than the glow on his face
is the fact that no-one contradicts him.

Ros Schulz

A Horror Tale

From an article in the *Observer*
following Hurricane Katrina, 2005

I think they are inhuman
but they still think they are human.
        My sleek grey sides
glisten with silver as droplets tumble
and I gambol in the dolphin pool.
My intelligence is so high
the CIA in their science fiction dreams
translated to reality
have trained me to attack divers
and enemy submarines:
implanted missiles in my sides.
But one day huge winds arrived
and monstrous waves.
We were washed to sea
three dozen bobbing corks
left to our own devices.
Our bosses, being without morals,
forgot to teach us loyalty.

Rae Sexton

The Prosperous Nation

Life is about change, Fiona.
'It wasn't meant to be easy.'
You must have known, Fiona,
when you became a cleaner for us—a small firm—
that you couldn't coast along forever on $18.75 an hour.
You must have known, Fiona, that
Aussie cleaners—true blue—are among the lowest paid.
Be proud, Fiona, that we're now offering you $12.75 an hour.
Or we'll have to let you go. Redundancy. No packages.
Yes, I know, Fiona, that you have worked conscientiously for us
for five years, no sickies,
but Australia is moving into the WORLD ECONOMY,
up with the big players, globalisation,
to create a prosperous nation.
We must economise, Fiona. Workers' wages.
The wage we are offering you is a reduction of only 33%.
Yes, you will have to change your lifestyle.
Give up the car. Use public transport. It's less polluting.
Eat less food. You'll get healthier.
Don't buy books. Save your eyesight.
Sacrifice your home. You'll have more money without the mortgage.
For a prosperous nation, Fiona. Stop crying. Don't be unreasonable. Be fair.
We'd like you to stay with us. Fair go. Be a part of my prosperity—
oops, OUR prosperity. Australia's prosperity, Fiona.
Think positive. It's a reduction of 33%. Less tax to pay.
Let's move into an economy of prosperity. Together, Fiona.

Alice Shore

Silent Village Streets

white wash
sea captain houses
fishermen huts slumber
rambling plums and
rosehips entwine
picket fences
a young girl
cycles in zigzags through
fallen leaves and apples
sea wind spreads salt
across sand grass
to wood pines

Lidija Šimkuté

Sun Splinters

blue tipped pines
burgundy maples
and saffron birch
mushrooms blush
in lichen bed
dew rolls from moss
wood velvet
a squirrel's dart
wakens
the gravel path

Lidija Šimkuté

We've burnt the midnight oil

We pretended not to notice
just how late it'd gotten.
Always today never tomorrow:
perpetually quarter to twelve.
No eye on the clock:
as we drive to the shops;
as we use our dryers;
tape those puerile shows;
as Industry's giant fists pummel the ground;
as we constipate rivers and seas;
as our last gasps of air leak these punctures
we ride the world
stubbornly down to the rim.
We buckle the wheeling world.
The taco cannot be wound back.
We didn't read the clock correctly.
Lady Midnight had long gone
We are alone at 1:20 am.

Alice Sladdin

S'No White

Mirror, Mirror on the Wall
couldn't you have fooled them all?

Where's the effing victory
if I'm only looking good to me?

Mirror, Mirror on the wall
damn your lying ill-lit gall.

Mirror, Mirror you savage crit,
oh, Whoopsa. Have you slipped?

Mirror, Mirror on the floor,
doesn't hurt me anymore.

Alice Sladdin

The Wounded Christ

I have met the wounded Christ:
he lives in Baxter.
He has fierce eyes and a strong body.
He says proudly that he comes from a *hard* culture
constantly resists and looks for ways of escape.
He is scornful
of a culture where an old man is not treasured
where families do not live together and girls
leave home
where there is no room at the table for more.

He lifts his shirt and shows us
deep razor-wire slashes that run
from one side of his body to the other,
huge weals across his ribs
over his heart,
it is hard not to avert our eyes.
(Later, while he is talking he runs his fingers over them
absent-mindedly soothing
and relearning the contours of his body.)

He takes off his jumper
when my husband shivers in the cold wind
gives it to him and will not accept its return
when we are to leave.
This is how we are he says.
We do not give something and then take it back.
If we give, then it is forever.

Pauline Small

Difference

I remember the first time
I entered an Asian deli—
they had six ducks
asleep on the gallows;
six lives over
in the flick of a wrist.
And I thought:
How brave those Asians are
to look their food in the eye.

Ian Smith

those moments

it's in those moments
when i'm caught
between touching you, and
not touching you,
and finding out that the truth
doesn't always move
the narrative along
that my life takes on the
orchestration of a car accident.

it's in those moments
when i keep finding the wrong
way to express myself
that i get the feeling i'm
a tourist here,
in my own town,
in my own home,
in my own bed.

it's in those moments
when i'm pushing
myself too far, but somehow
it's never far enough
and the burden of
carrying ugly
is just a knife slice
short of too heavy . . .

it's in those moments.

Kerryn Tredrea

Wheelchair

The orderly has pushed me to a square of grass
beside a path, in silence.
There is lots of noise, movement flashing, swirling
around, above.
But no words.
People hustle past, swinging name-tags from
confident necks,
and folders, briefcases for all who belong—
Doctors (ye shall know them by their stethoscopes)
shining in noon light.
Patients, a little bewildered, move forward
clutching their right to be here, jackets against
threatened rain, comforted with scents of home
and walking the dog.
On this path, everyone moves forever to somewhere,
coming and going.
Mothers and babies, little Batman or Crows
in bright Guernsey
shuffling, ceaseless sounds of sneakers, comfy
walk shoes, high heels teetering in their gloss.

Only I seem still, waiting for what?
Unnoticed in my square wheelchair
held in by big wheels in a square of grass
I can study cigarette butts, leaves, bottles, papers
very untidy.
But my wheelchair is tidy, neat metal pieces for
my feet. Brake on.
I mustn't fall out
I would be noticed, my passive observer
status lost.

But I can continue to notice things:
seagulls scuttering about, grabbing snacks
in the grass.
A fellow with one leg stumbles—
Perhaps he needs a wheelchair
he could share mine, bring lunch for both
of us.
I could find room in my tidiness for him.

Two magpies strut, aloof, keep their
distance.
Magpies would never contemplate a wheelchair.

I am not aloof, not going anywhere.
Want to wriggle free onto soft damp grass
become a nuisance underfoot.
I could take a can opener to my container,
pour myself out
throw myself down, land maybe on the
grimy concrete path.
give cause for litigation.
It won't happen
I snuggle back in my chair, glancing out.

If I smile, might someone smile back?
Wait for the orderly to come, wait by the path,
by the buildings, the edge of life.
There I can breathe in the air, squirm, grasp at glances
aim to collect just one smile.

Maureen Vale

Blue Shoes

Scuffed suede shades of blue
turned green-grey;
they smell of rain
and running for trams
of cobbled backstreets, wandering aimless
of surprise turns, discovery
of Melbourne.
I bought them the week I moved here:
new shoes for a new city.
Bright blue, they whistled softly
from their corner of a Brunswick St window
and I, beady bower bird, could not walk past.
I tested them out on the streets
round my new home—going nowhere
in particular, but everywhere is somewhere
or it seemed so that day.
They were light on my feet
soft rubber soles whispered to my skin
the shapes and sensations of each new step.
They took me to work
-the reason I moved-
they walked me home the night I quit.
They rode with me
the nine hour bus to Adelaide;
drew circles in the dust
as I tried to explain.
By then the first hole was opening
they didn't look so blue.
Still they got me back to Melbourne
and together, we scuffed those same streets
going nowhere, no longer exploring new places
instead noticing how they'd changed.
I thought about moving back to Adelaide:
I didn't. I got a new job
but left the blue shoes home.

They live by the back door now
tired and scungy—no good in the rain
though still comfortable.
They take me places like the corner store
or post office; sometimes
we even go nowhere
for old time's sake.

Amelia Walker

no secrets

he said there were to be no secrets
between us
I took him at his word
opened the door of my closet
bravely my skeletons marched out
one by one
exposed to daylight they crumbled to dust
I felt my foundations shudder and crack
more skeletons came out
ones I didn't even know
the cracks widened—shattered
I fell to pieces
he had no key to lock the closet door
and didn't know the secret
of how—to put the pieces back

G M Walker

Cats in tacks. Cat sin tax. Cat syntax. *

Awake and slow arch stretch
turn an almost go-round
        widen eyes
cry out to upstraight-walkers
still lying on sink-in mat

check out notdarkening eat-stuff box
        it purrs unopening
end of long sleepingtime
warmbright comes up
warmstriping the walk-on.

stretch, fur-warming.
Later, heat-stripes moved,
upstraight walker will unclose box

in the not-moving hold-still
memory-moving
pictures of the silver shine
under-the-water flashers

bring water to mouth
we catch them with claws
that flash silverfast

the same taste comes in the
round silver-hard cup
we cannot bite open

straight-walkers open
round with silver teeth held
        in notcat paws

we not-move still as rock
ground-jaw quivering
then pounce
faster than locust, lizard, bird.

this light-rising
we sit
wait
in their
food-warming place

stare at the not-darkening box
                        waiting

rob walker

*It is not widely known that cats have their own verb-based language.

The Sausage Factory

The machines of the sausage factory
Whinge, Whine and Moan
As they rip apart little piggies
Bone by bone

The sausage factory men
All gather round
To speed up the production
Of the bacon machine that they've found

And the bosses all sit in rows
Of chairs made of sausage,
Cause they haven't realised
Just how much they smell—pppphew!

You see the workers won't tell them
It's a terrible thing
Cause if they speak up
There'll only be mashed potato for tea

So the sausage men
     Sit
On their sausage made thrones
As middle management
Tries to emulate them like drones

But they got it wrong
They bought chairs of cheese
Which brought rats to the factory
Bringing the sausage tycoons to their knees!

So now the company is trading
From an overseas location
Cause the tariff's too high
On sausage and bacon

So no matter where you are
Or what you do for a job
Watch out for those who smell like cheddar cheese
And try to suck knob

Cause although factories are protected in a tax-free haven
The rats are still out
And they're hungry for big sausage
And ENORMOUS bacon.

Grant Walton

Untitled

I've defrosted
3 oysters

I'm going to have them
with

wasabi
wine
& Bukowski

Life is sweet
sometimes.

Daniel Watson

Digital Alarm Clock

High tech guillotine decapitates my timeless dreaming.

Dennis Wild

Group Therapy

Only when we stopped talking did I realise how silence can be
so inclusive.

Dennis Wild

Adelaide Winter

With our leafless frangipani looking like some Dali-esque hat stand
gone troppo.

Dennis Wild

Log Off

From the tangled forest of left-brained bedlam
I tread the healing pathway
homewards.

Dennis Wild

Edge of the World

the jetty
blistering black
was too hot for our young feet

like well-practised commandos
we inched along the side rail
dodging gut stains
jagged notches and salty scales

an abandoned tangle of hooks and line trailed away
whispering goodbye from the horizon

screeching gulls
circled whitely above
and a prickle-chinned man grinned
as silver gar flashed in his bucket

dad's holler was barely heard above shushing waves
but it was time to go

we inched back to shore
and that night
dreamed
of mermaids
and treasure

Brett Stuart Williams

Forest Hill Track

What Force is this, that blocks my forest track?
That hurtles at it rocks, like giants might do,
And throws upon it broken bough and branch?

This track leads up to where I keep my bees,
Which gather honey from the hillside's trees;
It is no threat to old lives such as these,
Intent on reaching up to sun and moon;
Or to this hill of Dreaming bones and stone.

Some Power, it seems, would wish to see me go,
And bars my way—not as boys might do,
Or wind and rain—but darkly, in the night.

So I must go with iron bar and axe,
To prise aside each rock, to chop and drag;
While trees crowd round, to whisper, watch and wait,
And sullen slopes so slowly grit and grate.

My grandson sometimes helps me clear the track;
'Why don't they like you, Gramps?' he asked today,
'This hill? These trees?—why do they block your way?'
And I replied, 'It's just the wind and rain.'

I could have said, 'There's ancient Forces here,
Which hate this track and want to see me gone,'
But I replied, 'It's just the wind and rain.'

They're in the hill's old bones; they wait, they lie,
They're in the rocks, they're in the forest's sigh.

'Why don't they like you?' he had wisely asked;
'It's just the wind and rain,' I'd replied.

'It's just the wind and rain.'

George Woolmer

the bombay café

friday at the bombay café
the gourmet talks ballet with his valet
between the pâté, the satay and the entrée
cliché after cliché after cliché.
the gay valet sips rosé
studies the inlay of the parquet walkway
bored with talk of the plié and the coryphée
he stares at the ashtray
contemplates croquet, payday and broadway
of being faraway in a santa fé cabaret.
the gourmet drinking beaujolais straightens his toupée
bumps the waiter and a tray of soufflé ricochets
on the pathway
in the mêlée the gay valet says he really can't stay
waylaying his parfait he makes for the foyer
the bombe gourmet relays his dismay
but says okay, see you on monday.
the blasé valet says 'you may'
and without delay heads for the parkway
to make his getaway
picks up his coupé, a chevy corvette, and speeds up the
driveway
to the highway and his weekend hideaway, faraway
far from the passé gourmet, per se.
on the freeway mind in disarray,
starting to stray like a mental replay, a teleplay resumé
he sees the hombre in a hallway in monterey
wearing a bouquet and a crochet beret.
he sees the chalet holiday in norway
with the divorcée and her fiancée who liked it both ways
dressed in a cutaway bouclé negligée
foreplay in the bob-sleigh, olé!
a risqué threeway interplay.

he sees the reggae deejay from zimbabwe
who nay could say neigh to some horseplay
they lay in the hay drinking dubonnet
lamé glistened in the midday sunrays.
he sees the kinky calais coutourier on the stairway
vibrating bidet, yelling obey! obey!
the attaché of the u.s.a in taipei resembled hemingway,
codename stingray, who went astray and one grey may
day
was betrayed by the c.i.a., to his dismay
which released a dossier of hearsay on his sexplay.

he sees soirée after soirée after soirée
and curses the day at the sickbay, the random survey
which led to the x-ray, the immunoassay and the doctor
communiqué
for more tests on wednesday, his nerves start to fray
he prays that that day will be his good news day
he prays that that day will not be his doomsday.

at the bombay café the gourmet
gets up to pay, and falls against the papier-maché
archway
helped through the doorway into the laneway he sways
he dreams of his heyday as a matinée devotée
he sways in mental decay, a social castaway
empties a throwaway sachet of fabergé
the spray leaves a trail from the alleyway to the subway.

far away in a footscray take-away
a modern day protegé of rabelais
au fait with roget and wordplay
drinks café au lait and surveys the passing array
day after day after day.

Komninos Zervos

Acknowledgements and Notes
by or about contributors

David Adès' poem 'Paper' was published in *ArtState*. He is an Adelaide lawyer, poet and occasional short-story writer. His poem 'Measuring the Man' in memory of Ray Stuart, was published in *FS Poets Thirty*.

Gaetano Aiello, a legal practitioner, and Treasurer of FS, is co-editor of *Friendly Street Reader 32* to be launched in 2008.

Liz Allan's poem 'Quitting'—a reminder of the power of addiction.

Yahia al-Samawy, a guest reader at Friendly Street, read his poems in Arabic: rob walker read the translation by Eva Sallis. 'Four Loaves from the Heart's Oven' was first published in *Two Banks with No Bridge* (Picaro Press, 2005). His poem 'Leave My Country' was chosen for the May FS website.

Jude Aquilina enjoys moon-gazing, writing poetry and going to FS meetings. Her poem 'Humbucking Heaven' was chosen for the March FS website.

Maeve Archibald's poem 'Lunch hour' won the FS mystic poetry competition.

Henry Ashley-Brown, studying Creative writing at Adelaide University, enjoys reading at FS.

Avalanche, aka Ivan Gabriel Rehorek—Owns several saxophones, mostly housetrained. Him too.

Elaine Barker, whose poem 'In Verona' appeared in *ArtState #15*, enjoys reading at FS and the commitment and friendship there.

Bruce Bilney brings his passion for conservation to FS.

Karen Blaylock: published in *The Canberra Times*, *Quadrant*, *Heat*, *Famous Reporter* and in Adelaide.

Mary Bradley, a prize-winner at the Salisbury Writers' Festival, won the August Poetry Slam, at Ubud, Bali.

Kate Bristow, English teacher, is the author of *See It While You Live*.

Brian J. Brock: Science teacher (Adelaide, Papua, Zambia, Pitjantjatjara Lands); fan of Roland Robinson, Wang Wei . . .

Steve Brock has been chosen for *Friendly Street New Poets 12*. 'Visions on the Gleneg Tram' was chosen for the July FS website

Belinda Broughton, a visual artist, has recently been concentrating on poetry. 'Poetry is a cow' was published in *Artstate #17*.

John Brydon is a Research Scientist at the University of South Australia. His poem 'Bloody Spring' was chosen for the February FS website.

Anne Chappel grew up in Tanzania, recently returned to writing and poetry.

Betty Collins: born 1928, still trying to come to grips with the world.

Dawn Colsey, published by *SOPHIA*, finds poetry distils inner and outer worlds.

Sue Cook, a recently retired hills dweller, has had poems published in
FS Reader and *Opinion*.

David Cookson: co-edited *FS Reader 22*, one of three in *FS New Poets 2*.

Veronica Cookson says, 'Yes, yes, yes! I've finally done it.'

Judy Dally, published in nineteen *FS Readers*, loves the sea, music,
teddy bears.

Jo Dekok, who, at 24, cares for others' kids, has been writing forever.
rdekok teaches at the Rosebud Writing Workshop in the
Adelaide Hills.

Jo Dey, a psychologist, would rather be a poet, published in many
FS Readers.

Kalicharan Nigel Dey, born 1951, believing the author impedes the poem,
prefers mystery. 'And I shall go', a translation of 'J'irai' by M.J. Moreas
(published 1886), was published in *Artstate #17*.

Genevieve Grace Drew has appeared in *FS 30, 31* and the Noble House
Publication 2004.

Tess Driver sings, watches whales, is published in Australia and overseas.
Her poem 'The society of the endangered poet' appeared in *ArtState #15*.

Garth Dutton has read regularly at FS for the last twenty years.

Peter Eason: mystic poet, co-edited *FS Reader19*, his latest collection *Journey
to Anima*.

M.L. Emmett: Academic, Anglo-Celtic, atheist wordsmith living in Kaurna
land, is co-editor of *Friendly Street Reader 32*. Her poem 'The forensic
science of grief' was chosen for *ArtState #16*.

Steve Evans and Kate Deller-Evans are writing the history of Friendly Street.

Margaret Fensom: 'Bridges' will be published in *Friendly Street New Poets 12*.
She has written since childhood and crossed many bridges in her travels.

Cameron Fuller, chosen for *Friendly Street New Poets 11*, is doing his PhD at
UniSA. His poem 'sometimes, meanings' was chosen for the December
FS website.

Juan Garrido-Salgado's 'Sonnet' appeared in *ArtState #15*. Coming from
Allende's Chile, his poetry cries out for justice for all who are oppressed.

Jill Gloyne, author of *The Nautilus Shell . . .*, was chosen for *FS's New Poets
Nine* in 2004. 'Adelaide in Autumn' was chosen for the August FS
website.

Jill Gower published in previous *FS Readers* is an active contributor to the
Hills Poets. 'Poets on Popeye' was published in *ArtState #17*.

rory harris: his most recent collection is *Songs* 2003. 'Semaphore' was
published in *The Peninsula*.

Geoff Hastwell, author of *My Sky Blue Trades*, brings his guitar, his songs and
his passion for justice to Friendly Street.

Roger Higgins has brought different parts of the world to FS in his poems.

Sally Ann Hunter: 'My writing lives me.'

Indigo, a professional writing student at TAFE, appears for the second time in a *Friendly Street Reader*.

Shirley Ireland, of the Riverland and Mallee Writers, occasionally reads at FS.

Patricia Irvine: 1947 Boomer. Jock. Aesthete. Black humour. 'Obituary' was chosen for the October FS website and 'Snake' for the next *ArtState*.

Rosemary Jaensch: Two books *Caught out being human* (2001), *Still Bemused* (2004)

Rob Johnson, from England via NSW in 1958, has written his poetry in Adelaide.

Erica Jolly's 'A villanelle for today' was commended in the FS 2006 political poetry competition.

Cheryl Jordan is rediscovering a pre-adult penchant for poetic pondering.

Khail Jureidini, reading at FS since 1975, has a special way with words.

Geoff Kemp, co-editor of the *FS Reader #20*, won the inaugural Seaview Poetry Prize in 2005. His poem 'Tracking' has been chosen for the next *ArtState*.

Michael Kingsbury, published in previous *FS Readers*, always surprises.

Jules Leigh Koch says his poems are written in the commercial breaks of life. 'The Port Noarlunga Hotel' had been accepted for publication by *The Canberra Times*.

Donna Kouis, a first time reader at Friendly Street.

Mike Ladd of Prospect, produces and presents 'Poetica' on Radio National every Saturday at 3.05 pm. 'Housing Estate in the Howard Era' was published in the *The Best Australian Poems 2006* (Black Inc).

Stephen Lawrence, poetry editor for *Wet Ink*, was a guest reader at FS. 'The Legislative Assembly' was commended in the 2006 FS political poetry competition. 'Science haiku' has been chosen for the November FS website.

Jayne Linke (Lynx): 'Walking' was published in *ArtState #14*. She has read at Friendly St and at the High Beam Disability Festival

K*m Mann—Two cats circle K*m's ankles as she writes her novel.

David Mortimer believes that each poem invents its own form. His poem 'Collecting' was chosen for *ArtState #14*.

Glen Murdoch, former consultant editor to *SideWaLK*, co-edited *FS Reader 21*.

Louise Nicholas co-edited *FS 30*: 'Threshold' won the 2006 Poetry Unhinged Competition. Her poem 'On writing poetry: capturing the essence' was chosen for *ArtState #16*.

Juliet Paine, at 27, aspires to breakdown misconceptions about poetry through her teaching and writing.

Ioana Petrescu, widely published, is the Director of UniSA's Poetry and Poetics Centre.

Barbara Preston also writes scripts and children's fiction. Her collection *Entering the arc*, was published in 2005

John Rice: 'Johnny's fireside chat' won the 2006 FS political poetry competition.

Alice Riedl, a poet for whom English is her second language.

Graham Rowlands: an Adelaide-based poet, published widely across Australia since the late 1960s. 'Doing something' was published in *Social Alternatives*, 'Long-suffering' has been accepted by *Woorilla*.

c m runnel: second year at FS, she completed HBCA at Flinders this year.

Ros Schulz's poem 'Flying Visit' was published in *ArtState #15*. She is published here and interstate: her focus is on relationships and landscape.

Rae Sexton: 'A Horror Tale' was read at the 2005 December meeting by Elaine Barker who wrote the eulogy for her in *Southern Write*. Despite decades fighting illness, Rae Sexton made a major contribution to South Australian writers, supporting the Sunday Prose Readings. She and her husband, Bob, published the anthologies of the group.

Alice Shore: My anger with the Howard Government fuels my political poetry. 'The Prosperous Nation' has been accepted by *Overland*.

Lidija Šimkuté, an international poet, guest reader at FS, writes in Lithuanian and English. Her poetry has been translated into eleven languages. Her collection *Thought and Rock*, with a foreword by J.M. Coetzee will be published in 2007.

Alice Sladdin won the Bundey Prize for poetry at Adelaide University, 2005.

Pauline Small writes when passion strikes: it struck with shame at Baxter. 'The Wounded Christ' was chosen for the April FS website.

Ian Smith says 'Thank God for those who seek beauty in all the darkest corners.'

Kerryn Tredrea: People need Poetry. An 'out there' poet, she's performed interstate and at local poetry slams. 'Don't' was published in *Artstate #17*. Her poem 'running with knives on a slippery surface' was published in *The Best Australian Poems 2006* edited by Dorothy Porter, published by Black Ink.

Maureen Vale: 'Wheelchair' was read at the November 2006 meeting by Louise Nicholas. Maureen's funeral was attended by the many poets who were her admirers and her friends. Her poetry is noted for its sensitivity and self-deprecating humour.

Amelia Walker: returned briefly to Adelaide. 'Blue Shoes' was in *ArtState #14*.

G M (Gail) Walker: 'no secrets' was published in *Blue Woman* by G M Walker (Bookends Books 2006) rob walker's collection of poems *micromacro* won the Poetry Unhinged competition. His 'Elegy for Colin Thiele' appeared in the *AEU Teachers' Journal*. His poem 'A beginner's guide to postmodernism' was chosen for *ArtState #15*.

Grant Walton: G Dubya is a performance poet and musician—contact walton.grant@gmail.com

Daniel Watson's poem 'Untitled' was published in *ArtState #16*.

Dennis Wild presented FS with one liners, experiments from a poetry workshop.

Brett Stuart Williams, born in Adelaide, is presently a captured spirit, writing for escape.

George Woolmer delights in the challenge of writing all kinds of poetry. His poem 'Forest Hill Track' has been chosen for the next *ArtState*.

Komninos Zervos, of Queensland, read at FS in the '80s, returned with 'the bombay café' this year.

For further information about
Friendly Street and its publications visit
www.friendlystreetpoets.org.au
Email: poetry@friendlystreetpoets.org.au
Postal: PO Box 43, Rundle Mall, Adelaide SA 5000